READING ABOUT

Baby Animals

by Janet Allison Brown

Aladdin/Watts
London • Sydney

Contents

© Aladdin Books Ltd 2000

Designed and produced by
Aladdin Books Ltd
28 Percy Street
London W1P 0LD

First published in
Great Britain in 2000 by
Franklin Watts
96 Leonard Street
London EC2A 4XD

ISBN 0 7496 3964 4

A catalogue record for this book is
available from the British Library.

Printed in UAE
All rights reserved

Editor
Jim Pipe

Literacy Consultant
Rosemary Chamberlin,
Oxford Brookes University
Westminster Institute of Education

Design
Flick, Book Design and Graphics

Picture Research
Brian Hunter Smart

If you were a baby animal, what would you like to be? Some babies, like baboons, spend most of their time close to their mother.

Crocodiles and ducks start life in an egg, and some babies are just full of surprises!

Baboons

Would you like to be a puppy dog?

Puppy

Puppies play with each other and bark, "Woof woof!"

Puppies curl up next to their mother's body and drink her milk. Then they go to sleep.

Drinking milk

Would you like to be a zebra foal? That is a baby zebra.

A foal gallops across the grass. The sun shines on its stripy coat.

The hair on its neck is called a mane. It blows in the wind.

Zebra foal

A foal's hard feet are called
hooves. Can you see them?

Would you like to be a lion cub? It has soft fur all over its body. Its mother carries it to a safe place and feeds the cub her milk. When it is bigger the cub learns to hunt.

Mother lion

8

Lion cub

Can you see its paws?

Here is a baby elephant, called a calf. Its long nose is called a trunk. This picks up grass and makes a sound like a trumpet.

Elephant calf

An elephant calf lives in a big family of elephants. It stays close to its mother – there might be a lion about!

Joey

Where is its body?

Would you like to be a baby kangaroo, a joey? Joeys stay really close to their mother – snug inside her pouch!

Bouncing

When they get older, they bounce along on two big feet.

13

Would you like to be a baby gibbon and swing through the trees? A baby gibbon hangs on tight. It does not want to fall.

Baby gibbon
It hangs on to its mother.

Here is a baby duck, called a duckling. A duckling starts life inside an egg. Its mother lays her eggs in a nest.

Duckling

Ducklings grow and grow until the egg breaks. Soon they can run and swim.

Egg breaks

Swimming ducklings

17

Would you like to be a baby penguin? It lives in cold places.

Chick

Penguins

18

Penguin chicks grow inside an egg. Their parents keep the eggs warm with their body.

All the chicks have brown fur. Can you see them in this picture?

Here baby crocodiles break out of their egg. They have very sharp teeth!

Baby crocodiles

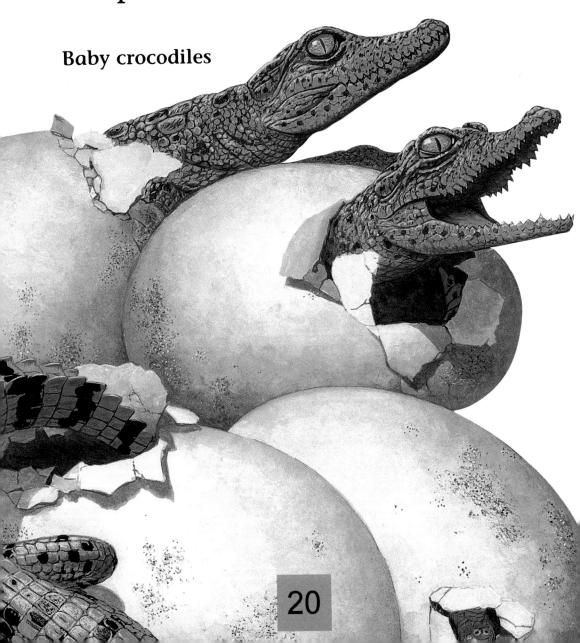

Mother crocodile

Crocodiles are born in a nest. Their mother carries them to the water in her mouth.

The babies soon learn to swim and catch other animals.

21

Tadpoles are baby frogs. They start life in eggs called frogspawn.

Frogspawn

When a tadpole leaves its egg, it has a big tail and lives in a pond.

Tadpole

A tadpole's legs
start to grow
and its tail
gets shorter.
Soon it is a little frog!

Growing legs

Frog

23

Baby spiders

How many legs
have they got?

Some animals have hundreds of babies. Look at all these little spiders!

Would you like to be a butterfly?
It would be very interesting.

A mother butterfly lays eggs on
a leaf. Out of each egg comes a
little caterpillar.

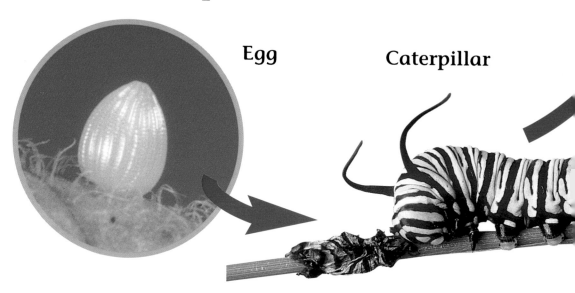

Egg

Caterpillar

The caterpillar eats and eats –
and eats! It grows big and fat.

Cocoon

The caterpillar makes a bag called a cocoon. Inside, it changes. When the cocoon opens, surprise! Out crawls a butterfly!

Butterfly

Can You Find?

Some baby animals have fur. Others have feathers or a smooth skin. Can you find which baby animal these skins come from?

A

B

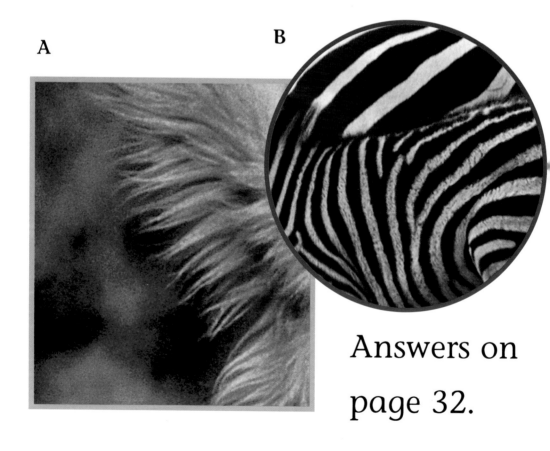

Answers on page 32.

C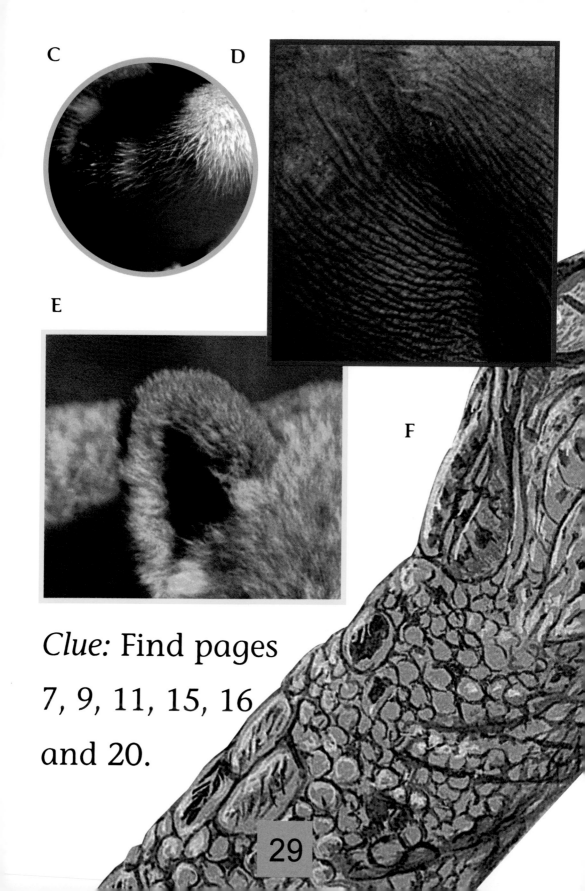

D

E

F

Clue: Find pages
7, 9, 11, 15, 16
and 20.

Do You Know?

Do you know these animals? Can you guess which of them lay eggs?

Snake

Budgie

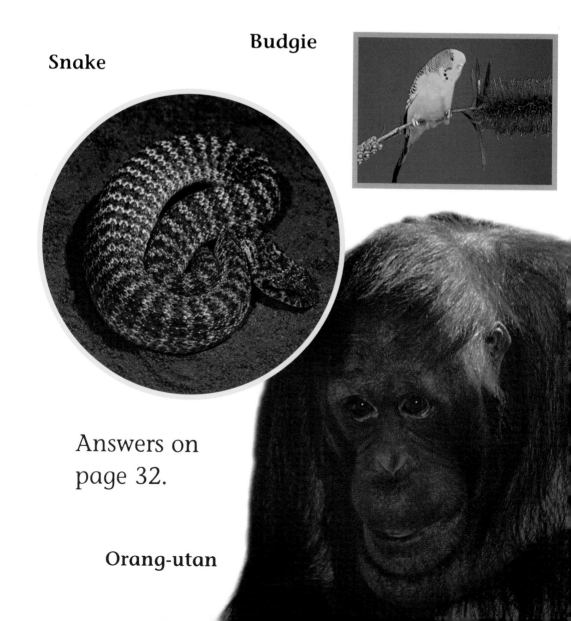

Answers on page 32.

Orang-utan

Dolphin

Hen

Grasshopper

Frog

Index

ANSWERS TO QUESTIONS

Page 28-29 – **A** shows a gibbon's fur • **B** shows a zebra's coat • **C** shows a duckling's soft feathers • **D** shows the skin of an elephant • **E** shows a lion cub's fur • **F** shows a crocodile's scaly skin.

Pages 30-31 – **Snakes** are reptiles and lay eggs like a crocodile • **Budgies** and **hens** are birds and lay eggs like a duck • **Orang-utans** and **dolphins** don't lay eggs. They have babies like a dog • A **grasshopper** has eggs like a butterfly • A **frog** lays eggs.

Photocredits: Abbreviations: t-top, m-middle, b-bottom, r-right, l-left, c-centre. Cover, 2tl, 2ml, 6-7, 10-11, 18c, 18-19, 23, 28mr, 29tr, 30 all, 31t, 31ml, 31br—Digital Stock. 1, 17, 31mr—J. Foxx Images. 3, 9, 29ml—Corbis. 2ml, 26mr—S.Moody/Dembinsky/FLPA-Images of Nature. 4, 28bl—Select Pictures. 12—D.Hosking/FLPA-Images of Nature. 14-15—Gerard Lacz/FLPA-Images of Nature. 16, 29tl—Stockbyte. 21—Brake/Sunset/FLPA-Images of Nature. 22t—W.Meinderts/Foto Natura/FLPA-Images of Nature. 22b—A.J.Roberts/FLPA-Images of Nature. 24-25—Silvestris Fotoservice/FLPA-Images of Nature. 26ml, 27b—L.West/FLPA-Images of Nature. 27tl—Treat Dividson/FLPA-Images of Nature. **Illustrator:** Chris Shields—Wildlife Art Ltd.